SO-BDQ-119

INSTANT PROGRAMS

FOR YOUTH GROUPS

From the Editors of Group Publishing

Loveland, Colorado

List of Contributors

Anderson, Timothy R.
Burns, Jim
Feldmeyer, Dean
Fisher, Karen J.
Parolini, Stephen
Pierce, Todd
Roehlkepartain, Eugene C.
Roehlkepartain, Jolene L.

Schultz, Joani
Searl, Bob
Smith-Farris, Jim
Tozer, Tom
Visker, Mary Ann
Warden, Michael D.
Woods, Paul
Yount, Chris

Instant Programs for Youth Groups 4
Copyright © 1990 by Thom Schultz Publications, Inc.

First Printing

All rights reserved. No part of this book may be reproduced in any manner whatsoever without written permission from the publisher, except where noted in the text and in the case of brief quotations embodied in critical articles and reviews. For information write Permissions, Group Books, Box 481, Loveland, CO 80539.

Credits
Edited by Michael D. Warden
Cover and book designed by Judy Atwood Bienick
Illustrations by Rand Kruback

Scripture quotations are from the Holy Bible, New International Version. Copyright © 1973, 1978, 1984 International Bible Society. Used by permission of Zondervan Bible Publishers.

Library of Congress Cataloging-in-Publication Data
(Revised for vol. 4)
Instant programs for youth groups.
   1. Church group work with teenagers. 2. Church group work with young adults.
    I. Group Publishing. II. Instant programs.
BV4447.I495 1988   259'.2   87-36874
ISBN 0-931529-32-8 (pbk. : v. 1)

1-55945-010-X   **Instant Programs for Youth Groups 4**
Printed in the United States of America

CONTENTS

INTRODUCTION

"What am I going to do with the youth group this week?"

"How can I find creative activities to do with my group?"

"How can I plan unique experiences for my kids with a minimal amount of preparation?"

In response to many youth leaders' requests for help, Group Publishing's editors have compiled this resource. *Instant Programs for Youth Groups 4* offers a multitude of creative, meaningful activities—all combined into one handy resource. The meetings require minimal preparation. They include step-by-step instructions on what to do and how to do it. They also offer quality handouts that are ready to copy, a great help for busy youth leaders. In addition, each session provides "Bonus Ideas" that allow youth workers to help kids dig deeper into topics that interest them.

This resource includes practical, proven programs from TEENAGE Magazine's Leaders Guide, plus expanded and adapted articles from TEENAGE Magazine. The programs concentrate on the needs and concerns faced by today's young people. Program topics include AIDS, crime, spiritual growth, school stress, busyness, steroids, teen pregnancy, drinking, prayer, Bible study and the occult.

As you use these timely programs, watch your young people grow in their relationships with God and others. Notice how they interact in discussions and respond to the involvement activities. Watch your young people develop a personal faith that will be the basis for a mature adult faith. Exploring and questioning faith issues within a supportive environment allows your young people the chance to see God at work in themselves, others and the world.

So open the book. Pick a topic. Get ready for an exciting meeting. And be prepared to experience God at work in your life and the lives of your young people as you use this special resource—*Instant Programs for Youth Groups 4*.

7.95

SECTION ONE:

Tough Topics

 1. Home Street Home

Purpose:

To inform your kids about the plight of homeless people and how to help them.

Session outline:

1. Before the meeting—Plan to have the entire meeting outdoors during a cool evening. Be sure to have blankets handy and candles for light. Or if possible, set up a barrel outside with old newspapers or pieces of wood in it. Light the contents and use it as a source of light and heat.

2. Refreshments?—Open the meeting by distributing refreshments. Give one apple and three potato chips to each person. Serve only water to drink.

Materials:
- ☐ two or more blankets
- ☐ three or more candles
- ☐ matches
- ☐ Petra's album, *On Fire!* (Sparrow/Star Song)
- ☐ stereo
- ☐ newsprint
- ☐ marker
- ☐ Bible

For each person:
- ☐ apple
- ☐ three potato chips
- ☐ glass of water

3. Just imagine—Read aloud "Greg's Story." Ask:

● **What does it feel like to be cold and hungry?**

● **After this meeting you can all go home to warm beds and full refrigerators—but how would you feel if you couldn't?**

4. Homeless sculpture—Form small groups. Have the groups walk around and find items they can use to make a sculpture that represents how homeless people must feel. Suggest they look for things such as old pop cans, candy wrappers and other trash. After groups have created their sculptures, form a circle and ask each group to describe what its sculpture represents.

5. Shelter the homeless few—If possible, get a copy of the song "Homeless Few" from Petra's album, *On Fire!* (or something similar). Then ask:

- **How does this song make you feel?**
- **What's our responsibility for helping homeless people?**
- **What would Jesus do for homeless people?**

6. Biblical commands—Ask someone to read aloud 1 Corinthians 4:10-16. Ask:

- **What is Paul's message to the church at Corinth in this passage?**
- **Paul mentions he is homeless, hungry and poorly clothed—why does he want the Corinthian church members to be imitators of him?**
- **What can we learn from Paul's words?**

Read aloud Matthew 25:31-46. Ask:

- **What is Jesus commanding in this passage?**
- **How does it apply to us?**

7. Actions speak louder than thoughts—Have someone read aloud "How You Can Help the Homeless." Then ask:

- **How can you be like Trevor?**
- **What can our youth group do to help the homeless?**

List suggestions on newsprint. Then discuss with the group which step to take first (donate clothing, food, dental-hygienic products). Challenge group members to go directly from the meeting and follow through with that action. Offer a brief prayer and read aloud Proverbs 14:21 as a closing statement and a challenge.

Bonus Ideas!

- **Citywide help for the homeless**—Go around the city collecting blankets, food, clothing, toothbrushes and toothpaste to give to the homeless. Advertise the pickup day in your local newspaper and at shopping centers. Involve other youth groups for a broader impact.
- **Fund-raiser profits**—Make a group decision to contribute 10 percent of the money raised by your group's fund-raisers to a local or national charity that helps homeless people. Persuade other youth groups to do the same. You'll discover the money adds up fast after just a year.

Greg's Story

Seventeen-year-old Greg stands on the cracked concrete steps and looks around. He sees people rummaging through a nearby dumpster. He watches a woman through a broken window cook a can of food over a hot plate. Inside a doorway, two guys stick needles into their arms.

Greg has just come home from school. He has never brought a friend home with him, nor does he want to. He doesn't want anybody to see where he lives.

Greg and his family live in a homeless shelter. At night, Greg sleeps in a room with 400 beds. Sometimes the snoring from his roommates keeps him awake late into the night.

Greg and his family struggle to survive each day. When they're hungry, they pick through the garbage for a cold, half-eaten hamburger. When they get dirty, they don't know when they'll bathe. A park fountain substitutes for a shower.

When Greg gets bored, he doesn't find much to do. "All you do is put on the radio. Turn off the radio. Put on the radio. Turn off the radio," Greg says.

Before school, Greg wakes up early to rush down to the street corner. Each day a city newspaper truck stops by to hire people to sell newspapers during the early morning rush hour. Greg usually earns enough money to buy a bag of chips or a soft drink for lunch.

After peddling papers, Greg dashes into his first class as the final bell buzzes. Greg avoids getting to school any earlier because he hates the embarrassing reminder of being homeless.

"People tease me at school," Greg says. Then he stops talking. The muddy, frayed, hemless pant cuffs and the wrinkles permanently etched into his shirt finish Greg's sentence. Greg doesn't own nice clothes, or clean ones.

Greg's disheveled appearance only reminds his classmates that not all teenagers have money—or a home.

Greg and his family once had money and a place to live. But Greg doesn't like to talk about that. He only says how the landlord evicted them one day because his mother couldn't pay the rent.

"Last year we were on the streets," Greg says as he picks at the dirt trapped under his fingernails. "We were there at Thanksgiving, and we were there at Christmas. Do you know how bad that is?"

Greg then sits back and surveys the chipped buildings and litter-filled empty lots. "I'll feel good about myself once I earn my keep," he says. "I just gotta find something to do."

How You Can Help the Homeless

Trevor Ferrell gives homeless people hope. When he saw a news report about the homeless, 11-year-old Trevor knew he could do something.

And he did. After grabbing a blanket and a pillow, Trevor persuaded his family to drive 15 miles to downtown Philadelphia.

After driving around, Trevor spied a man huddled over a grate. Trevor got out of the car and gave the man a soft pillow and a warm blanket. Then he went home.

But the next night Trevor didn't stay home. He and his family delivered hot food to the homeless. Eventually a religious organization donated a 33-room shelter, which is now named "Trevor's Place."

Today while Trevor attends a Quaker boarding school, his family and volunteers run the shelter in Philadelphia that Trevor started when he was 11. During the day, volunteers help the homeless find full-time work and a permanent place to live.

Like Trevor, you too can help the homeless.

● **Pray**—Pray for people such as Trevor who work with the homeless. Then pray for the homeless.

● **Volunteer**—Your community may have a homeless shelter, a soup kitchen or a food bank that needs your help.

● **Organize friends**—Collect blankets and together with your friends give them to the homeless on the streets.

● **Set up a clothing drive**—Collect hats, scarves, coats, gloves and sweaters. Although these items don't seem necessary in summer, as soon as the evenings become cooler, the homeless need protection from the cold. Give collected items to an organization that helps the homeless.

Whatever you do for the homeless—even if it's small—helps.

"One person can make a difference," Trevor says. "Just do what you can and follow your heart."

2. SEDUCED BY STEROIDS

Purpose:
To help kids discover that the effects of drugs such as steroids seem to make life better but actually have negative consequences.

Session outline:

1. The scoop on steroids— Distribute copies of "The Scoop on Steroids" quiz to group members and have them each mark their answers.

Then tell kids the answers: (1) True, (2) True, (3) False, (4) False, (5) True, (6) True.

2. Pumping air—Have a "muscle" contest. Ask for three or four volunteers to go into a separate room and place balloons under oversized sweat suits to form "muscles." Then have them come out one at a time and "pose" for the rest of the group. Have the group vote for the winner of the contest by applauding.

3. Steroids and "air"-oids discussion—Ask:

● **How are the air-filled-balloon "muscles" like the muscles produced from steroids?**

● **Is it surprising so many high schoolers are using steroids? Why or why not?**

● **Why do guys often want to use steroids?**

● **Do athletes have to use steroids to compete effectively?**

Materials:
☐ 24 balloons for "muscles"
☐ three or four sweat suits
☐ Bible

For each small group:
☐ permanent marker

For each person:
☐ copy of "The Scoop on Steroids" quiz
☐ pencil
☐ balloon
☐ pin

Why or why not?

4. A drug is a drug—Form small groups. Give each group three of the balloons from the contest and a permanent marker. Have groups write "Alcohol" on one, "Cocaine" on another and "Steroids" on another. Then have group members discuss the differences and similarities of each of the drugs.

Ask:

● **How does the drug harm you physically?**
● **Why do people use (or abuse) the drug?**
● **What's the lure of the drug?**
● **How does the drug make people feel? What are the potential dangers of the drug?**

5. Facing temptation—Read aloud Proverbs 1:10-15; Matthew 26:41; and 1 Corinthians 10:13, 28-32. Ask:

● **What do these scripture passages say about temptation?**
● **How can God help you avoid the temptation to use steroids in order to "look good"?**
● **What are better ways to feel good about yourself than using steroids or other drugs?**

Read aloud Psalm 139:13-18. Say: **God loves you for who you are now—not who you become by using drugs.**

6. Beat the temptation—Give each person a pin and balloon, and reread Psalm 139:14. Have kids pop the balloons at the same time to symbolize conquering the temptation to abuse drugs such as steroids.

Bonus Ideas!

● **No-steroids campaign**—Have teenagers form a campaign to inform the students in their high school(s) of the dangers of steroids. Have a fund-raiser to get enough money for posters, pamphlets and a guest speaker.

● **Muscles without drugs**—For those teenagers who want to develop muscularity, form a club that meets to work out on a regular basis. Help these kids develop a format for each workout that includes a brief "spiritual workout" (Bible study) in addition to a physical workout.

● **Scriptural "uppers"**—Have teenagers look up verses in the Bible that build their self-worth and encourage them to do their best, such as Psalm 139:13-18; 145:18-19; and 2 Timothy 1:7. Have kids write these on little slips of paper and put them in old pill bottles. Encourage them to use these "scriptural uppers" whenever they need to build their self-esteem muscles.

The Scoop on Steroids

Instructions: For each of the following statements, write true or false.

True or False?

1. Using steroids is an easy way to build muscles fast. _____

2. You become more aggressive when you use steroids. _____

3. If you use steroids and do not lift weights, you'll still get bigger muscles. _____

4. You can gain 50 pounds of muscle weight within one month if you use steroids. _____

5. Some teenagers take steroids to improve their looks, not to become better athletes. _____

6. Longtime steroid abusers have died of liver tumors, heart attacks and strokes. _____

Permission to photocopy this handout granted for local church use. Copyright © 1990 by Thom Schultz Publications, Inc., Box 481, Loveland, CO 80539.

3. Victimized!

Purpose:

To help teenagers understand how to respond if they become victims.

Session outline:

1. Eye-opener—Read aloud "Black Eyes, Bruises and Stolen Cars." For each item, have group members make a fist if they're surprised by the fact and cross their arms in front of them if they aren't surprised.

2. What do you do?—Form small groups. Give each group a "Case Study: Revenge or Justice?" handout, paper and a pencil. Have groups each read the handout and discuss the questions. Then have groups each list situations in which people are victims. Have groups each discuss how someone might respond with revenge or justice. Ask:

- **How are justice and revenge alike? different?**
- **Do you often feel tempted to fight back? Why or why not?**
- **Do you ignore the situation? Why or why not?**
- **What are good responses to situations where you're victimized?**

3. Fighting back—Form pairs. Give each pair two balls of clay. Without allowing any talking, give partners each two minutes to mold a shape that represents how he or she might feel as a victim. While one partner molds the clay, have the other watch silently. Then have partners switch roles. Ask them to briefly discuss how it felt to express feeling victimized.

Ask:

- **Is it easy to express the feeling of being victimized? Why or why not?**

Materials:

For each small group:
- ☐ copy of "Case Study: Revenge or Justice?" handout
- ☐ paper
- ☐ pencil

For each person:
- ☐ modeling clay
- ☐ Bible

4. Biblical advice—Have partners to read Exodus 21:23-25 and Matthew 5:38-42. Have them discuss:
- **How do these verses differ?**
- **If you turn the other cheek, is justice served? Why or why not?**

Have partners read Romans 12:17-19. Have them discuss:
- **What do these verses say about seeking revenge? justice?**

5. Clay cross—Have kids each place their clay "victims" in the center of the circle to form a cross. Pray with group members for understanding of what justice means in each situation they encounter. Close the meeting by thanking God for the strength to overcome the feelings of victimization.

Bonus Ideas!

- **Professional advice**—Invite a local professional counselor who deals with victims of serious crimes to talk with your group. Compile an anonymous list of group members' questions before the meeting.
- **Pamphlet**—Get copies of "Protecting Yourself Against Crime" by J.L. Barkas, pamphlet #564 from Public Affairs Pamphlets, 381 Park Ave. S., New York, NY 10016-8884.

Black Eyes, Bruises and Stolen Cars

Your car stereo disappears during a wrestling match. You fight with your best friend and end up with a bruised arm. Being a victim happens much more than we think. According to *The Youth Ministry Resource Book* (Group Books):

● Half of high school seniors say something worth less than $50 has been stolen from them within the past year.

● Teenagers are more likely to be victims of crimes than any other age group. Those least likely to be victims? The elderly.

● About 40 percent of victims of violent crimes know their assailant.

● Forty-three percent of teenagers say they've experienced some form of physical violence at home.

● Each year, one of every 15 teenagers becomes a victim of a violent crime.

● About 30 percent of high school seniors say they've been threatened by someone.

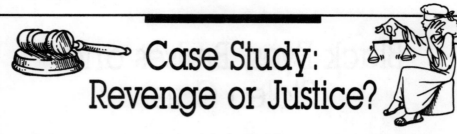

Case Study: Revenge or Justice?

Jesus said in the Sermon on the Mount: "I tell you, do not resist an evil person. If someone strikes you on the right cheek, turn to him the other also" (Matthew 5:39).

But is there a difference between revenge and justice?

Let's say Bob tells an awful lie about Greg. And Greg decides to fight back by spreading untrue rumors about Bob. Is that justice?

According to the Bible—no. The Apostle Paul said, "Do not repay anyone evil for evil. Be careful to do what is right in the eyes of everybody" (Romans 12:17).

Greg wanted revenge, not justice. His goal was to get even. But that still leaves a question: What is justice?

For Greg to seek justice, he should've confronted Bob directly about the lie. A good thing for him to say would've been: "I've heard that you said I got drunk last night. I feel hurt. I wanted to come right to the source and find out if you really said that. And I wanted to let you know that it's not true. I spent the evening at a concert with my family.

Did you say I was drunk?"

Questions:
● When was a time you wanted revenge? justice?

● How would Greg confronting Bob about the lie achieve justice?

● What other ways could Greg have responded to achieve justice?

● How did you respond in your situation—with revenge or justice? Explain.

Permission to photocopy this handout granted for local church use. Copyright © 1990 by Thom Schultz Publications, Inc., Box 481, Loveland, CO 80539.

4. Christians and Drinking

Purpose:
To help kids think intelligently about the use of alcohol.

Session outline:

1. Happy-Hour Game Show— Play the Happy-Hour Game Show. Form two teams and appoint a captain for each. Explain that you'll read a question and then ask team A for its answer. Use questions from the "Booze, Abuse and Happy Hour" game sheet. For example, "What percentage of high school seniors surveyed say they've drunk alcohol sometime in their lives?" After getting a percentage from team A, ask team B if it thinks the percentage is higher or lower. If team B is right, it gets a point; if not, team A gets the point. Alternate between teams until you've asked all the questions. Award canned root beer to the winners.

2. Diving into the froth— Form groups of three or four. Distribute the "What Does the Bible Say?" handout to each person. Assign each group one of the Bible verses listed in the handout. Ask groups to read their verses and discuss how the verses help make decisions on whether drinking is okay.

3. Don-a-who?— Using a pencil or pen as a "microphone," walk around the room like a talk show host. Ask individuals:

Materials:
For every other person:
- ☐ one can of root beer
- ☐ pencil or pen
- ☐ tape
- ☐ party supplies

For each person:
- ☐ Bible
- ☐ beer-bottle-shape paper
- ☐ copy of "What Does the Bible Say?" handout and "Quotable Opinions" handout

- **Is it okay for Christians to drink? Why or why not?**
- **What did the scripture passages tell you?**
- **Are the scripture passages relevant to today's culture? Why or why not?**
- **Why do so many kids drink? Are the reasons valid?**

4. Checking your position—Give each person a "Quotable Opinions" handout. While still acting as a talk show host, read aloud each quote. After each quote, ask individuals to explain why they agree or disagree with it.

5. Tough questions—Give each person a Bible and a beer-bottle-shape (see pattern on page 21). Have kids read the verses listed in the "What Does the Bible Say?" handout. After they read all the verses, have them write "Always," "Sometimes" or "Never" on the beer-bottle-shape paper, depending on when they think it's okay for a Christian teenager to drink alcohol. Have kids tape their bottles to the wall in categories. Discuss people's opinions.

6. Supporting one another—Gather in a circle. Read aloud 1 Peter 2:13. Ask group members to consider what this verse says about teenage drinking, since it's against the law. Then ask:

- **What role does peer pressure play in teenage drinking?**
- **What role does rebellion play?**
- **Does the fact underage drinking is illegal make a difference? Why or why not?**
- **How can teenagers help each other overcome the pressures?**

7. Party without alcohol!—Have a party. Provide food, drinks, music, games and other activities to show alcohol isn't necessary for a fun time.

Bonus Ideas!

- **Alcohol to the extreme**—Ask a speaker from Alcoholics Anonymous to visit the group. Have group members prepare questions in advance. Ask the speaker for tips on how to keep alcohol from controlling someone's life.

- **Try these**—Get *Controversial Topics for Youth Groups* by Edward N. McNulty (Group Books) and look at Issue #2 ("Should parents accept the reality of drinking, but make a covenant with their children not to drive after drinking?") Also get *Drugs, God & Me* by Kathleen Hamilton Eschner and Nancy G. Nelson (Group Books) and *What Teenagers Are Saying About Drugs & Alcohol* by Chris Lutes (Tyndale House Publishers).

What Does the Bible Say?

The Bible's a great place to see for yourself. Check out these verses and use them to help you make a decision about drinking alcohol.

1 Timothy 5:23

Judges 13:3-5

Ecclesiastes 9:7

Ephesians 5:18

Luke 1:15

Titus 2:2-6

John 2:1-11

Isaiah 5:22-23

Permission to photocopy this handout granted for local church use. Copyright © 1990 by Thom Schultz Publications, Inc., Box 481, Loveland, CO 80539.

Quotable Opinions

Is it wrong for Christians to drink alcoholic beverages?

"I think anything (done) in excess can be harmful including food, driving too fast and talking too much."
Wendy Williams, 12
Knoxville, Tennessee

"Yes. I don't know anybody who's benefited from drinking alcoholic beverages. But I know that many people have been hurt by it."
Jeremy Johnson, 13
Basalt, Colorado

"I think it's okay as long as it doesn't become an obsession. Jesus himself drank wine."
Rusty Carlton, 15
Sterling, Virginia

"Yes, because you're destroying the Lord's temple."
Michael Goucher, 15
Pineville, Louisiana

"No. Alcoholic beverages don't always have to be associated with alcoholism and don't *have* to be an addictive drug. Christian teenagers could show that you can *enjoy* a drink rather than drink to excess."
Sonja Boon, 18
Fort Saskatchewan, Alberta, Canada

"I think it's okay as long as you don't abuse it."
Paul Tessmer, 18
Deerwood, Minnesota

Permission to photocopy this handout granted for local church use. Copyright © 1990 by Thom Schultz Publications, Inc., Box 481, Loveland, CO 80539.

Beer-Bottle Pattern

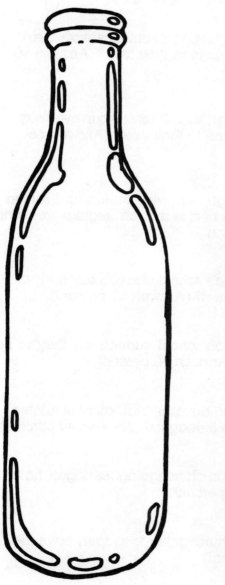
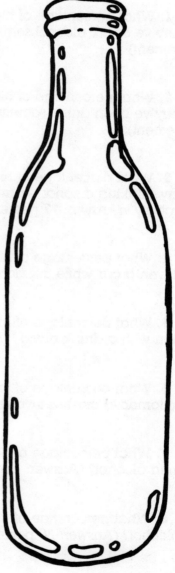

Permission to photocopy this handout granted for local church use. Copyright © 1990 by Thom Schultz Publications, Inc., Box 481, Loveland, CO 80539.

Booze, Abuse and Happy Hour*

1. What percentage of high school seniors surveyed say they've drunk alcohol sometime in their lives? (Answer: 90 percent)

2. What percentage of high school seniors surveyed say they've been drunk sometime in their lives? (Answer: 66 percent)

3. What percentage of high-achieving juniors and seniors say drinking alcohol is part of a teenagers' regular weekend activity? (Answer: 77 percent)

4. What percentage of high school students say they've driven a car while intoxicated? (Answer: 57 percent)

5. What percentage of high school students say they've ridden with a drunk driver? (Answer: 80 percent)

6. What percentage of the nation's fatal, alcohol-related automobile crashes involve teenagers? (Answer: 40 percent)

7. What percentage of non-churchgoing teenagers have tried alcohol? (Answer: 88 percent)

8. What percentage of churchgoing teenagers have tried alcohol? (Answer: 80 percent)

*Answers taken from *The Youth Ministry Resource Book*, published by Group Books.

5. A Teenage Father's Story

Purpose:
To take a serious look at the responsibilities and problems of teenage fathers.

Session outline:

1. Congratulations, you're a father!—Invite two young fathers to help with the meeting.

As kids arrive, hand the guys each a raw egg and a marker. Explain that each guy is now a "dad," and his egg represents a new baby each was recently "blessed" with. Have guys each decorate their new "child." Ask guys each to take care of their baby for the rest of the meeting. (Watch and take note of the girls' reactions.)

2. Game time—Have the group play volleyball. If dads put down their babies, have the real fathers call the dads out of the game periodically to take care of their "crying babies." Be sure to call each dad out of the game at least once.

3. Responsibilities of fatherhood—Sit in a circle and give kids each a piece of paper and a pencil. Have them each draw a line down the middle of their paper. On one side, have them each write a brief schedule of what they've planned for the next week (at school, home or elsewhere).

Materials:
- [ ] equipment for volleyball
- [ ] recording of a popular lullaby (optional)
- [ ] stereo (optional)
- [ ] egg carton

For each guy:
- [ ] raw egg
- [ ] marker

For each person:
- [ ] piece of paper
- [ ] pencil
- [ ] copy of "Father Knows Best" handout
- [ ] Bible

When everyone is finished, ask them how their activities might change if they had a baby to care for. Have them each write a revised schedule on the other side of the paper.

Occasionally refer the following questions to the real fathers for their responses. Ask:

- **What changes take place when you have a baby?**
- **Is it better to wait to have children? Why or why not?**
- **Why do most teenagers believe getting pregnant "won't happen to me"?**

4. Father knows best—Give each person a "Father Knows Best?" survey and a pencil, and have group members each mark their response.

When everyone is finished, collect the surveys, tally the results and read them to the group. Then read aloud the "How Do You Compare?" box.

Ask kids whether the survey results or the "How Do You Compare?" information surprises them. Briefly discuss the pros and cons of each option listed on the survey.

5. Checking out the Bible—Form small groups and give each group one of the following verses:

- Genesis 2:24
- Romans 13:13-14
- James 1:12
- Psalm 127:3
- Titus 2:6-7

Have groups read and discuss what the verses say about premarital sex and responsibility.

6. How to put off being a dad—Gather everyone in a circle and ask the groups to briefly explain their findings. Then ask the role-playing dads to talk about what it's like to be totally responsible for another person.

Ask the guys:

- **How did you feel knowing that the girls didn't have to help with your "baby" in any way?**
- **What do you think a guy's responsibility should be in a teen pregnancy situation?**

Ask the girls:

- **How did you feel about the guys having to care for the kids?**
- **How is this experiment different from the way life usually is? Explain.**

Ask the group:

- **What is the only foolproof way to avoid becoming a teenage dad?**

7. Egg carton—Close with a prayer: **Thank you, Lord, for parenthood and for giving us the wisdom to know its place in our**

lives. Give us the strength to follow your guidelines for responsible sexual behavior. Amen.

Sing or play a record of a popular lullaby as the dads place their babies to sleep in a waiting egg carton.

Bonus Ideas!

● **Real-live teenage dad**—If possible, invite a teenage dad to your meeting. Have group members prepare questions ahead of time. Talk about the changes that come about when a teenager becomes a parent.

● **A report and a poster**—Order the report "Declining Earnings of Young Men: Their Relation to Poverty, Teen Pregnancy, and Family Formation" or a black-and-white poster with the title "An extra seven pounds could keep you off the football team" from Children's Defense Fund, 122 C St. N.W., Washington, D.C. 20001.

How Do You Compare?

In a survey of teenagers by Teenage Research Unlimited, 46 percent of guys and 53 percent of girls said, "I would get married and keep the baby." Thirty-one percent of guys and 18 percent of girls said they would handle the pregnancy by abortion. Fifteen percent of girls and 12 percent of guys said they would keep the baby but not get married. Fourteen percent of girls and 12 percent of guys said, "I would give up the baby for adoption."

Father Knows Best?

What would you do if you got a girl pregnant or you became pregnant? Checkmark the option you'd most likely choose. Squiggle out your last choice.

☐ I would give up the baby for adoption.
☐ I would get an abortion.
☐ I would keep the baby but not get married.
☐ I would get married and keep the baby.

Permission to photocopy this handout granted for local church use. Copyright © 1990 by Thom Schultz Publications, Inc., Box 481, Loveland, CO 80539.

6. Buy! Buy!

Purpose:
To stimulate kids' thinking about materialism.

Session outline:

1. Before the meeting—Prepare the meeting room to look like a catalog showroom. Set up a "display window" on one of the walls: Tape to the wall pictures and descriptions of items such as sports cars, vacations, stereos, musical instruments, televisions and other expensive items. Include the prices in the descriptions.

2. Money for nuthin'—As group members arrive, hand each a paper cup filled with 25 pennies. Announce that you've just been informed their pennies are the last ones on Earth. Because of this, each penny is worth $1,000. Tell the kids the items in the display window are now available for the amount shown on the descriptions.

Say: **You may spend some, all or none of your pennies on the items in the display. If you choose to spend the money, give it to me and I'll give you a slip of paper listing the items you purchased. There is an unlimited supply of each item.**

After kids have purchased items, ask:

● **Why did you buy what you did?**
● **Why did or didn't you spend all your pennies?**
● **What would you do with the leftover pennies (if there are any)?**

3. What should I buy?—Ask:

Materials:
☐ retail catalog pages
☐ masking tape

For each small group:
☐ Bible
☐ newsprint
☐ marker

For each person:
☐ paper cup
☐ 25 pennies
☐ slip of paper
☐ dollar-size piece of green construction paper

● **Does money guarantee happiness? Why or why not?**
● **What's important to you that money can't buy?**
● **Why is it important to you?**
● **Do "things" cost you more than just the money it took to buy them? Explain.**
● **Is worrying about *not* spending money as bad as focusing on spending money? Why or why not?**

Discuss why people are drawn to the lifestyles of rich and famous people. Ask:

● **What kinds of images do the "rich and famous" portray?**

4. Materialism—Form three groups. Give each group one of the following passages: Proverbs 11:23-28; Matthew 19:16-26; and Luke 6:21-25. Have groups read and discuss the meaning of their scripture passages. Give groups each a large sheet of newsprint and a marker. Have each group write one or two sentences explaining the main point of the passage. Then gather everyone together and allow each group a minute to read and explain its sentence(s) while taping the newsprint to the wall.

Ask:

● **What's a common message of these three scriptures?**
● **Do they say it's bad to be rich? Explain.**
● **According to these scriptures, should rich people change their lifestyle or follow any particular guidelines? Explain.**

5. Fading away—Read aloud James 1:11. Explain that the value of the pennies spent earlier has just dropped due to an amazing discovery of millions of pennies collected from wishing wells all across the country. Say: **Unfortunately, your catalog orders haven't been processed yet. The store isn't going to honor your pennies' previous value.**

Collect the slips of paper and return the pennies. Discuss the feelings kids would have if they were wealthy and suddenly their wealth were taken away. Read aloud Job 1 and discuss how Job responded to losing everything.

6. What's right for you?—Give each group member a green piece of construction paper the size of a dollar bill. Hand out markers and have kids each decorate one side of the "bill" with words and pictures that represent how they can be responsible with their money. Ask them to include words that help them remember what the Bible says about riches. Then have them turn over the paper and list things that are free, such as friendship with God, love from others, sunsets. Have kids each write a brief prayer thanking God that the best things in life *are* free.

Close by having each person say his or her prayer aloud.

Bonus Ideas!

- **Discussing wealth**—Have kids prepare questions ahead of time about how to deal with wealth from a Christian perspective. Invite a wealthy member of your church to a meeting to discuss the questions. Or set up a panel discussion between two groups of church members—those who believe it's okay to be wealthy and those who don't.

- **Monopoly with a difference**—Play a marathon version of Monopoly with your group. Add two variations to the game: (1) At any time, a person may donate money to another person. He or she must explain the reason for the donation; and (2) Designate a bowl on the game board as "the work of the church fund." Explain that people may place money in the bowl any time. Set a time limit to the game. The winner is the person whose wealth is closest to the value of the "work of the church fund."

- **Materialism materials**—Look for these books: *Rich Christians in an Age of Hunger* by Ronald Sider (Paulist Press) and *The Mustard Seed Conspiracy* by Tom Sine (Word Publishing).

7. Spooks, Seances and Satanists

Purpose:
To uncover information about the occult and how Christians should respond.

Session outline:

1. Occult scavenger hunt— Meet at a shopping mall and arrange for transportation back to the church. Or if possible, hold the entire meeting somewhere near or in the mall.

Form teams of four to six. Give each group an "Occult Scavenger Hunt" handout and a pencil. Set a time limit for the scavenger hunt. Have groups each go through the mall, following the instructions on the handout. When they complete their handout, have groups each return to the starting point. The first team to return wins.

2. Food for thought— Award the winning team angel food cake and the losing team a dish of red-hot candies. Then discuss the handout discoveries. Ask:
- **What shocks you about what you're finding?**
- **What does God want us to know about the devil?**

3. Scripture hunt— Have group members read and discuss:
- Exodus 20:3
- Leviticus 19:31
- Deuteronomy 17:2-5
- 1 Chronicles 10:13
- Isaiah 47:13-14
- 1 Peter 5:84

Materials:
- ☐ angel food cake
- ☐ dish of red-hot candies
- ☐ napkins

For each group of four to six:
- ☐ copy of "Occult Scavenger Hunt" handout
- ☐ pencil

For each person:
- ☐ Bible

Ask:
● **What concerns you about the occult?**
● **Is there any connection between the occult of today and the demons of Bible times? Explain.**
● **Is it okay for a Christian to play with a Ouija board? Why or why not?**
● **Is it okay for a Christian to go to a horror movie? Why or why not?**

4. Focus on Christ—Have kids pair up and pray for strength. Give each person a Bible and have pairs read Ephesians 1:18-20. Conclude by reading aloud Ephesians 6:10-20.

Bonus Ideas!

● **Further reading**—Read *The Screwtape Letters* by C.S. Lewis (Fleming H. Revell Company). It's an excellent resource that deals with the reality of the devil in our everyday lives. Also get *Understanding the Occult* by Josh McDowell and Don Stewart (Here's Life Publishers).

● **Police advice**—Invite police to talk about what they see happening in your local community as far as the occult is concerned. Have them give advice for your group in helping overcome it.

Occult Scavenger Hunt

Do this discussion-starting scavenger hunt at a shopping mall near your church.

Find out the price of a Ouija board. $_____

How many Ouija boards has the store sold in the past month? _____

Find the AC/DC albums at a record store. How many times is the word "hell" mentioned in the titles of the songs? _____

Find Thrasher magazine (a skateboarding magazine). How many times does Satan's picture appear in the magazine? _____

Find the title of a book on palm reading. _____

Find the name of a book on witchcraft. _____

Name three publishing companies that publish horoscope or astrology books.
1. _____
2. _____
3. _____

Find out how many programs or games a computer store has that are like Dungeons & Dragons. _____

Find the price of a deck of tarot cards. $_____

Name two horror movies that are playing right now.
1. _____
2. _____

Find the zodiac sign of three people.

Sign	Person
1. _____	_____
2. _____	_____
3. _____	_____

Find three people who believe in ghosts.
1. _____
2. _____
3. _____

List three videos you can rent that have something to do with the devil or the "undead."
1. _____
2. _____
3. _____

Find *Understanding the Occult* by Josh McDowell and Don Stewart. How much does it cost? $_____

Look up Deuteronomy 18:9-14. In your own words, what does this say?

Do the same with Acts 13:6-12.

Write Acts 19:19.

Permission to photocopy this handout granted for local church use. Copyright © 1990 by Thom Schultz Publications, Inc., Box 481, Loveland, CO 80539.

8. Facing the Threat of AIDS

Purpose:
To calm fears about AIDS by informing teenagers about the facts.

Session outline:
1. News briefs—As group members arrive, give each person a newspaper page. Tell kids to tear the newspaper into a shape that describes how they feel about AIDS. Have each person share his or her name and the newspaper shape's explanation.

Say: **AIDS is all over the news. And like most news, it can be frightening. To face up to fears, it's always best to be informed. To inform everyone about AIDS, we'll play Jeopardy.**

2. Jeopardy—Have one or more volunteers lead a Jeopardy game with facts about AIDS. In Jeopardy, the answers are supplied—group members must supply the questions. For example: (Answer) Seventy percent of AIDS patients are this sexual orientation. (Question) What is homosexual or bisexual? Award 500 points for each correct question.

Use the "Jeopardy Fact Sheet" as a source for questions. Or use the resources listed under "Bonus Ideas!" to get more facts.

Encourage your volunteers to explain and host the game. Divide into three or four teams and have them each answer as a collective body. Have fun with it.

3. Getting serious—Set the mood for serious discussion by giving

Materials:
- [ ] copy of "Jeopardy Fact Sheet" handout for volunteers
- [ ] matches
- [ ] person with AIDS (if possible)

For each person:
- [ ] newspaper page
- [ ] candle
- [ ] Bible

each person a lighted candle and turning off the lights. Say: **We've had a lot of fun learning about this deadly disease, but there's a serious side to this too.**
   Ask:
   ● **What questions do you still have about AIDS?**
   ● **How should people respond to people with AIDS?**
   ● **Should Christian teenagers respond to the AIDS issue any differently from non-Christians? Why or why not?**
   4. Opening up—If possible, invite an AIDS victim (or someone who knows a person with AIDS). Allow time for that person to tell what it's like to have AIDS. Focus the discussion on people, not just issues.
   If you can't get a person with AIDS to attend your meeting, use the "Letter From Jeff" to prompt an AIDS discussion with your group. Read aloud the letter. Then ask:
   ● **Is Jeff's anger at healthy people justified? Why or why not?**
   ● **What have you discovered from this letter about AIDS that you didn't realize before?**
   ● **How has hearing this letter changed your perspective on people with AIDS?**
   5. Gospel scan—Give each person a Bible. Have kids each scan the Gospels, pointing out stories in Jesus' life that teach us how to respond to AIDS victims and to fears about AIDS. For example, look at the passage in Luke 6:37-42 about judging others and the story of the 10 lepers in Luke 17:11-19. Use a New International Version Bible or a similar one with subheads, which help highlight stories.
   6. Prayer—Extinguish all the candles but one. Pass the lighted candle around the group. When kids each receive the candle, have them say a prayer concerning AIDS and pass the candle to the next person.

Bonus Ideas!

   ● Visit with a hospital staff member. Ask questions about AIDS.
   ● Get AIDS basic facts. Order the "Teens & AIDS!: Why Risk It?" and "AIDS: Think About It" pamphlets. Both pamphlets may be ordered from Network Publications, Box 1830, Santa Cruz, CA 95061-1830.
   ● For updated information, contact the national Centers for Disease Control AIDS hotline: 1-800-342-2437.

Jeopardy Fact Sheet

1. Answer: Seventy percent of AIDS patients are this sexual orientation.
Question: What is homosexual or bisexual?

2. Answer: Having sexual intercourse, sharing intravenous-drug needles, receiving blood transfusions from someone carrying the virus.
Question: How is AIDS spread?

3. Answer: (Call the national Centers for Disease Control at 1-800-342-2437 for the most recent figures.)
Question: How many people have died of AIDS?

4. Answer: Not having sex or taking drugs.
Question: What is the best defense against contracting AIDS?

5. Answer: Kissing, holding hands, drinking from the same glass or water fountain, swimming in the same pool or using the same toilet.
Question: What are ways that AIDS is not transmitted?

6. Answer: Ninety-five percent recognize it.
Question: What percentage of people understand AIDS by name?

7. Answer: The age group from 14 to 25.
Question: What age group is the least well-educated about AIDS?

Permission to photocopy this handout granted for local church use. Copyright © 1990 by Thom Schultz Publications, Inc., Box 481, Loveland, CO 80539.

Letter From Jeff

My name is Jeff. I have AIDS. If I was seated next to you right now you'd probably get up and move away, even leave the room. People always do that to me when they find out.

I look normal—just like you. I don't have any horrible signs of the disease. But the tests were positive so I've been exposed to the AIDS virus. I already know what you're thinking: "Fooling around—that got him in trouble." Well you're wrong. I got this stinking disease from a blood transfusion several years ago when I had my appendix out. A lot of us caught it that way. They just didn't know how to test the blood. At least now they do.

I guess I'm eventually going to die from the disease. Do you know how that feels? Knowing something inside you is going to kill you one day. I hate it! I'm a bomb waiting to go off. Any day I could start showing signs of the disease.

Then, they tell me I may never show signs at all. How do you even begin to plan a life when you feel there's no life to plan? Nothing seems to matter. What good is it to set goals or plan a career or just to have a normal life? You just can't know how it feels to have this horrible thing inside.

I'm really scared. No one will listen to me. Everywhere I go people who know I have the disease run away. My parents moved because people were throwing rocks at our house. People left nasty signs on our front door and sent hate mail. You'd think I was a freak or something. Well, I'm not a freak. Doesn't anyone know how badly I hurt inside? I need someone to care.

You stupid people. You can't catch anything by being around me. Talking to me or going to school with me isn't going to give you AIDS. A handshake, a smile, a phone call . . . why can't you just show a little kindness?

Do you have any idea what it's like not having a friend . . . not even one? Maybe I should just end it all. That's what everyone seems to be telling me I should do anyway. You kill me with your fear and your hatred. You kill me with your isolation and your meanness. It's like you hope I go ahead and just do myself in so you don't have to worry about me anymore.

But you know what hurts most of all? Sometimes I think God doesn't even love me anymore. The way you Christians treat me tells me that. If you're supposed to be God's agents of love and caring and support, then why do you shove me away? Maybe God doesn't love me anymore either. What's the use of going on?

I don't know what to do to get you to care about me. Just a kind letter . . . a phone call . . . a simple conversation . . . how wonderful that'd be. But the best of all would be to have a friend again. I used to take friends for granted. Not anymore.

Would you be my friend? Would you be my friend?   *Jeff*

9. When Your Friend Has an Eating Disorder

Purpose:
To learn about eating disorders and how to have a healthy body image.

Session outline:

1. Spoon relay—Form two teams. Have teams each form a circle. If your group has five members or less, form a single team, do the relays more than once and time your team to beat its record. Give each person a spoon as a passing utensil. Give each team a bag filled with the following items to pass on a spoon: an egg, a cotton ball, a pingpong ball, a toothpick, a marshmallow and a playing card. See which team can pass all the items around its circle the fastest without dropping any items. Have a team start over each time it drops an item.

2. My image: upside-down or right-side-up?—Form a circle with each person holding a spoon. Explain the theme of eating disorders. On the count of three, have kids each display their spoon "scoop side" down or "scoop side" up. Then have kids each respond to the following statement, depending on whether their image in the spoon is upside-down or right-side-up. (A spoon reflects either, depending on

Materials:
☐ two identical bags, each filled with these items: an egg, a cotton-ball, a pingpong ball, a toothpick, a marshmal-low and a playing card
☐ Bible

For each person:
☐ spoon
☐ "Eating Disorder Quiz"
☐ pencil

which way you hold the spoon. Try it!)

Depending on your group, you may want to separate guys and girls for the following.

Say: **If your image is right-side-up, tell about a time you felt really good about your body. If your image is upside-down, tell about a time you felt really bad about your body image.**

3. The meat of the meeting—Give each person an "Eating Disorder Quiz" and a pencil. Have kids each complete the handout. Then go over the answers and discuss any areas where kids seem misinformed. Ask:

● **How do you know the difference between a weird food habit (such as eating jelly-covered marshmallows) and an eating disorder?**

● **How do you know when dieting has gone too far?**

● **What can you do if you suspect a friend has an eating disorder?**

4. Body Bible study—Read 1 Samuel 16:7. Ask:

● **Why are people so hung up on outward appearances?**

● **What hope does this verse give us concerning our body images?**

● **Does it mean God doesn't care how we look? Why or why not?**

● **What are ways we can start looking at hearts instead of outward appearances?**

Have someone read aloud 1 Corinthians 6:19-20. Ask:

● **How does this verse make you feel—proud? guilty? glad? frightened? Why?**

● **Why would God choose to have the Holy Spirit dwell in your body?**

5. Body buddies—Have kids pair up and tell at least one thing they admire about their partner. The praise could be for an outward, body-image characteristic or an inner, heart quality.

6. Spoon-fed prayer—Have kids bring their spoons and join in a circle. Ask each person to think of a friend who might be struggling with an eating disorder. Have kids each offer a spoken prayer for that person without naming them while placing the spoon in the center of the circle to make the shape of a cross. Say: **No matter what we think of ourselves, Jesus always loves and forgives us. He wants us to have a "cross-eyed" view of ourselves, seeing ourselves as he sees us.**

7. Good food to eat—Have volunteers bring an assortment of low-calorie, healthy snackfood, for instance, cheese, crackers, fruit and popcorn. Alert kids to nutritious ways of eating.

Bonus Ideas!

● **Distorted vs. real images**—Take the group to an amusement park with fun-house mirrors or to a pond, or use a plastic mirror that distorts a person's reflection. Let kids laugh and have fun examining their body shapes in their reflections. Discuss the parallels in how we see ourselves, how others see us and how God sees us.

● **Info for kids**—Order Public Affairs Pamphlet #632, "Anorexia Nervosa and Bulimia: Two Severe Eating Disorders" by Beverly Jacobson, Public Affairs Committee, 381 Park Ave. S., New York, NY 10016.

● **Counseling help**—Delve into pages 394 through 398 of Dr. G. Keith Olson's *Counseling Teenagers*, Group Books, Box 481, Loveland, CO 80539. That section explains the causes of anorexia nervosa and offers advice on ways to help.

Eating Disorder Quiz

Instructions: Write "T" or "F" beside each of the following statements to indicate whether you think the statement is true or false.

1. A person is first considered to be anorexic when his or her body weight drops to below 60 percent of normal. _____

2. Bulimics almost always "binge" alone. _____

3. You can usually pick out a bulimic by his or her appearance. _____

4. Anyone who looks thin should be suspected of anorexia. _____

5. Anorexics often suffer from insomnia and hair loss. _____

6. Bulimics sometimes suffer from poor teeth or swollen cheeks. _____

7. Anorexics and bulimics may often be moody or irritable. _____

8. People with eating disorders often spend lots of time with other people to help them not think about food. _____

9. The reasons people become anorexic or bulimic are known and understood. _____

10. It's best to be direct when confronting a friend about a possible eating disorder. _____

Answers: 1. False. A person is considered anorexic when his or her body weight drops below 75 percent of normal; **2. True.** Unlike anorexics—who are overly thin—bulimics may appear perfectly normal; **4. False.** Many people are naturally thin. An anorexic looks unnaturally thin and undernourished; **5. True.** **6. True.** **7. True.** **8. False.** Actually, people with eating disorders tend to withdraw from others; **9. False.** No one knows for sure why some people become anorexic or bulimic; **10. True.** It's important to let them know you're seriously concerned.

Permission to photocopy this quiz granted for local church use. Copyright © 1990 by Thom Schultz Publications, Inc., Box 481, Loveland, CO 80539.

SECTION TWO:

Me and School

10. "I'm So Busy!"

Purpose:
To help kids know when they've become too busy and how to keep from burning out.

Materials:
For each team:
☐ three to five permanent markers
☐ 15 same-color balloons
☐ three Bibles

For each person:
☐ copy of "Busy Quiz" handout
☐ construction paper balloon
☐ pencil

Session outline:
1. Juggling schedules—Form teams of five kids. Assign one person from each team to be a scorekeeper for the team. Give each team several permanent markers plus 15 balloons of the same color (different teams should have different-color balloons). Then have team members inflate the balloons and write something they're involved in (such as school, sports, a club, youth group, or a singing group) on each balloon. Say: **On "go," pick up all of your team's balloons and throw them in the air. The object is to keep your team's balloons in the air. You may use your hands, feet and head. If you grab a balloon or let one touch the floor or intentionally hit another team's balloon, your team gets a point. The scorekeeper for your team will keep track of these points. The team with the fewest points at the end of three minutes wins.**

2. Juggling time—Form new small groups. Ask:
● **How did you feel while you juggled the balloons?**
● **What was the most difficult part about trying to keep the balloons in the air?**
● **How is juggling these balloons like keeping up with everyday activities? How is it different?**

Give each person a "Busy Quiz" and a pencil, and have kids complete the quiz.

When everyone is finished, ask:
- **What was your score on the quiz?**
- **Does your score surprise you? Explain.**
- **How busy are you compared to your peers? Why do you think that is so?**
- **Why do people cram so much into their daily schedules?**

3. Putting balance back—Have everyone form a large circle. Place all the balloons in the circle. Give each person a construction paper balloon. Say: **List on one side of your paper balloon several activities you participate in. Then circle the activities that benefit other people; place a star by the ones you have to do; and place a smile next to the ones you do because they are fun.**

Ask:
- **Which activities do you have too many of? Explain.**
- **Which activities do you need more of? Explain.**

4. When Christ got tired—Request three volunteers and give each a Bible. Have volunteers each read aloud Mark 6:45-46; Luke 5:15-16; or John 4:4-6. Ask:
- **Why did Christ need to rest?**
- **Why do we need to rest?**

Read aloud Matthew 11:28-30. Ask:
- **How can God help us slow down in our busy world?**

5. Balloon reminders—Have group members each pick up a paper balloon that lists an activity they feel would give them balance. They may want to either add or cut back on the activity. Then have kids each write out Matthew 11:28 on the other side of the paper balloon. Encourage kids to keep their balloon reminders as long as they can.

Bonus Ideas!

- **Keeping balance**—Plan a monthly time for kids to get together and take the "Busy Quiz." Then have them discuss how they can regain balance in their lives if they have lost it—or simply rejoice in the balance they've found.

- **Plan it**—For each person, get a copy of the *Student Plan-It Calendar* (Teenage Books). Meet with teenagers each week to talk about the balance in their past and future schedules. Have kids write Matthew 11:28 on the inside front cover as a reminder of Jesus' promise to give rest to those who are weary.

Busy Quiz

Instructions: For each question, circle the letter that best describes your situation. Then determine your score using the information below.

1. How many colds have you had this school year?

    A. None or 1
    B. 2 or 3
    C. 4 or more

2. How many books did you read for fun in your spare time last year?
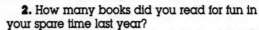
    A. 3 or more
    B. 1 or 2
    C. None

3. How many hours of sleep do you average each night?

    A. 8 or more
    B. 7
    C. 6 or fewer

4. How many meals did you eat with your family last week?

    A. 5 or more
    B. 3 or 4
    C. None to 2

5. How many times in the last month have you fallen asleep someplace other than in your own bed?

    A. None
    B. 1 or 2
    C. 3 or more

6. How many times in the last month have you had to hurry in the morning because you slept too late?

    A. None
    B. 1 to 5
    C. 6 or more

continued

7. How many times have you looked at your watch today?
- A. 0 to 5
- B. 6 to 10
- C. 11 or more

8. How many times this year have you canceled out on something you promised to do because you ran out of time?
- A. None
- B. 1 to 3
- C. 4 or more

9. How many times in the last month have you been surprised by a test or assignment grade that was lower than you expected?
- A. None
- B. 1 to 3
- C. 4 or more

10. How many arguments have you had with your parents this week?
- A. None
- B. 1 to 3
- C. 4 or more

Now figure out your score. Give yourself one point for each A you circled, three points for each B and five points for each C. Then add your total points. Use the scale below to evaluate your score.

10-17 Points

Yea! Your schedule isn't too busy. In fact, it seems like stress isn't a problem for you. But take time to evaluate your schedule. Is it balanced or do you spend a lot of time in front of the tube? If you feel good about your balanced schedule, give yourself a pat on the back. Congratulations!

18-26 Points

Not bad. You probably find that life clips along at a steady, yet challenging pace. Sometimes it gets extremely busy, sometimes it doesn't. Think carefully before you add other commitments to your schedule.

27-34 Points

You're busy. Sometimes, very busy. Your schedule stays full most of the time, and you're rarely bored. Usually you handle your many commitments pretty well. But sometimes you feel overwhelmed. Don't add anything to your schedule unless you drop an activity you're already doing.

35-50 Points

Whoa! While you may thrive under stress, chances are that you're overstressed and buried under commitments. Drop some commitments as soon as possible!

Permission to photocopy this handout granted for local church use. Copyright © 1990 by Thom Schultz Publications, Inc., Box 481, Loveland, CO 80539.

11. Working Backward to Get Ahead

Purpose:
To help kids get organized.

Session outline:

1. The missing piece—Form groups of four to six. Gather enough children's puzzles for each group to have one. But there's a catch: Give each group a puzzle with one piece missing. Have groups each complete their puzzles, except for the missing piece. For fun, allow no speaking during the task.

Once the kids realize they have a missing piece, talk about what they learned from this activity. Say: **Trying to reach goals in life is similar to piecing together a puzzle. If we don't have all the parts we need to complete the picture, we won't reach the goal. Paying attention to each of the parts is just as important as striving for the final goal.**

2. Getting organized—Have kids rate their organizational skills in different areas from 1 to 5, with 5 being the greatest. Read aloud each area listed below and have kids respond by showing the number of fingers for their rating. Areas:
- schoolwork
- youth group
- looking toward the future
- closet
- room
- (add your own)

Have each person choose one area to improve.

Materials:
- [ ] set of signs from the "Schedule Stations"

For each small group:
- [ ] children's puzzle, minus one piece

For each person:
- [ ] paper
- [ ] pencil
- [ ] year-long calendar

Starting at the back of the room and ending by the door, label areas of the room with the following signs that you cut apart from the "Schedule Stations" handout:
1. Set Your Final Goals First
2. Determine Your Final Goal Date
3. Set Weekly Goals
4. Set Daily Goals
5. Celebrate!

Have groups begin at the first sign. Supply paper, pencils and calendars for each person. Have kids each read the portion of the handout at each sign and think of how it applies to their goals. Have them complete each step and move on to the next sign.

3. A timely celebration—Have each person report his or her goal and timetable. Then divide the group in half, putting the two groups at opposite ends of the room. Then have teenagers back up toward each other until each person is back to back and links elbows with another. Have partners pray for each other and provide support as they work toward their goals.

Have someone read aloud Ecclesiastes 3:1-8. Conclude with prayer.

4. Check-up—Plan to check back with each person to see how the goals are being met. Have kids write their commitments so you could send a reminder in a month.

Bonus Ideas!

● **Calendar gifts**—Supply your youth group members with a *Student Plan-It Calendar*, (Teenage Books). It's complete with devotions and a calendar for planning.

● **More goodies**—For their personal devotion time along the way, offer kids each a *Grow For It! Journal* by David Lynn and Mike Yaconelli (Youth Specialties).

● **Plan a campout**—Have group members organize a camping trip. Delegate each of the planning responsibilities to a different group member. Then at the campsite, evaluate your group's organizational skills. Celebrate the successes. Then look for areas of improvement.

Schedule Stations

Instructions: Photocopy these five sections and post them each on the meeting-room walls as indicated in meeting.

1. Set Your Final Goals First

List the major long-term goals you want to accomplish within the next eight months. Think about your personality, your physical fitness, hobbies, activities, talents, homework, community projects and church commitments. Choose one goal to work on.

2. Determine Your Final Goal Date

Finding out your final goal date is easy when you're aiming to try out for an athletic team, music group or other group. But it's tough when you plan to lose weight, learn how to speed read or get in shape.

Make sure you give yourself enough time to reach your goal. For example, if you want to lose weight, most doctors recommend losing no more than two pounds a week.

3. Set Weekly Goals

Before you can make weekly goals, you need to work backward. Break down your long-term goals into smaller ones. For example, if you want to develop more friendships in the coming year, decide the steps you need to take to reach that goal, such as meeting one new person each month or becoming a pen pal with two new people in the next six months.

4. Set Daily Goals

Set a "one-step" achievement mark for yourself each day that will help move you toward your goal. For example, if your goal is to do better in English, set a daily goal to read 20 pages of the assigned novel. Or maybe commit to starting a journal to improve your writing skills.

5. Celebrate!

When you reach your goals, treat yourself to something special. Give yourself a pat on the back for making your "backward" organization system work.

Permission to photocopy these stations granted for local church use. Copyright © 1990 by Thom Schultz Publications, Inc., Box 481, Loveland, CO 80539.

12. Surviving School Stress

Purpose:
To discover why grades cause stress and ways to overcome that stress.

Session outline:

1. Stress pileup—Form teams no larger than four for a relay race. Divide each team in half, so two teammates stand facing the other two teammates, about 20 feet apart. All teams should stand parallel to each other. Give each person three books (hymnals work well and are uniform in size). Have one person run the distance to a teammate and hand his or her books to that person. That player then runs with six books to the next person and hands off the pile. The team that carries all 12 books to the finish first without dropping them wins. If a player drops a book, his or her team must start over.

Talk about the relay. Ask:
- **What made this stressful?**
- **How is that like school?**
- **Are you expected to carry a heavier load than you think you should? Why or why not?**

2. Report-card time—Have each person do "Your Stress Report Card." Discuss discoveries. Find out why some kids don't get as stressed as others.

Materials:
- ☐ soft background music
- ☐ stereo

For each person:
- ☐ three books (hymnals work well)
- ☐ copy of "Your Stress Report Card" handout and "Tricks of the Grade" handout
- ☐ pencil
- ☐ Bible
- ☐ paper

3. Stress review—Form groups of four. Ask the groups:

● **What's the most nerve-wracking part of school? Why?**

Suggest the person who took a test most recently begin sharing in the small group. Give each person a "Tricks of the Grade" handout and a pencil. Have each group read aloud the suggestions, then have them each circle three they need to work on most.

Have kids discuss within their groups:

● **Which three did you circle? Why?**

● **Which suggestions, if any, do you disagree with? Explain.**

● **What will you do to improve the three areas you circled?**

Divide Psalm 23:1-6 among the groups. Have groups each study its verse(s) by asking:

● **How can this verse apply to school and grades?**

● **How does this verse offer a suggestion for overcoming stress?**

Then ask each team to paraphrase its verse(s) to reflect school stress. For example, "Even though I've got three tests in one day, piles of homework and feel way behind, I know you're right there beside me, guiding me through it all." Have groups each present their verses by reading, singing or acting.

4. Making the grade—Have kids each write their name at the top of a piece of paper, then write these grades in large letters below their name: A, B, C, D, F. Have kids each pass their paper around the circle in their group. When kids each receive someone's paper, they must write five affirming and encouraging words to that person, each starting with a different grade letter. For example: Artistic, Bubbly, Caring, Dependable, Fun.

5. Put your heads together—Have team members form a circle on the floor by lying on their backs with their heads together in the middle. Take time to relax and be quiet. Play soft background music. Then read aloud Psalm 23 followed by Romans 12:3-8 as a closing prayer.

Before kids leave, make sure each person receives at least three back rubs from three different people.

Bonus Ideas!

- **Stress help**—Order "How to Handle Stress: Techniques for Living Well" from Public Affairs Committee, 381 Park Ave. S, New York, NY 10016-8884.
- **Tutor time**—Involve adults in the congregation as tutors. Find out what subjects adults feel comfortable helping kids with. Then match kids with adults who can help with their homework.
- **Parents in the know**—Invite parents to a youth meeting on grades. Give parents tips on being support people; give kids helps for communicating their stress to parents. Encourage parents to purchase *Helping Your Teenager Succeed in School* by Dorothy and Lyle Williams (Group Books).
- **Retreat on stress**—Plan a retreat or lock-in using *Group's Retreat in a Box™: All Stressed Out* by Joani Schultz and Stephen Parolini (Group Books).

LOOK ON THE NEXT PAGE

Your Stress Report Card

How well do you handle school stress? Grade yourself on how well you cope with these stressful situations. Give yourself an A if the situation doesn't cause you any stress. Or an F if the situation makes you completely stressed-out. Give yourself B's, C's and D's for the various degrees of stress between A's and F's.

1. Your math teacher throws a pop quiz. You're two days behind in your studies. _____

2. Tomorrow you're scheduled to give a speech about AIDS. You just can't get started. It's already midnight, and you still haven't written anything. _____

3. You hurry home from school to check the mailbox for your report card. But your dad got home early and has already seen it. _____

4. You need to get an A in history to make the honor roll. You get a test back and it has a C on it. _____

5. It's finals week. But all six of your teachers scheduled final exams on the same day. _____

Did you feel pressured to give yourself all A's? Did you give yourself grades higher than you should've? If so, you feel pressured to always make the best grades.

But if you feel you gave yourself honest grades, congratulations. You're beginning to recognize the effects of school stress.

Permission to photocopy this handout granted for local church use. Copyright © 1990 by Thom Schultz Publications, Inc., Box 481, Loveland, CO 80539.

 # Tricks of the Grade

Instructions: Read these suggestions, then circle three you need to work on the most.

● **Keep up with your schoolwork.** If you do assignments as soon as you get them, great! If not, set up a regular study schedule. Then stick to it.

● **Focus on learning, not grades.** Do more than memorize textbook answers. "If I feel I've learned all I could," Liana says, "I don't worry about what the test score says."

● **Ask for help.** When you don't understand something, ask your teacher. Or ask all your teachers about areas you need to improve.

● **Tell the truth.** If there's a reason for your poor performance, let your teacher know. Many teachers are understanding. "If a student goes to a teacher and says, 'My sister attempted suicide last night,' the teacher will make adjustments in the academic workload for that student," high school principal Bob Poirier says.

● **Talk with your parents.** Find out what your parents expect. Some teenagers think their parents want straight A's from them. But in reality, their parents only want them to do their best.

● **Set realistic goals.** Do you expect to get a 4.0 grade-point average? be the valedictorian of your class? go to Harvard or Yale?
  Are those expectations realistic? Solomon asked for wisdom and knowledge, not good grades. So ask yourself: "What am I doing here? What's the value of my education?" Then decide what performance you can be satisfied with.

● **Find your niche.** So you're not good at math. Have you written a creative story that blew your teacher away? Do you play solos in the band? Are you a whiz at fixing cars? Don't focus on your areas of weakness. Take joy in the gifts and talents God's given you.

● **Feel good about yourself.** Remember: God made you, and you're important. Study Romans 12:3-8. Think about your gifts. Use them. No matter what your grades, you're still a gifted creation of God.

Permission to photocopy this handout granted for local church use. Copyright © 1990 by Thom Schultz Publications, Inc., Box 481, Loveland, CO 80539.

13. Working Part Time: Is It Worth It?

Purpose:
To probe into the tough and terrific aspects of working part time.

Session outline:
1. Here's your resume—As kids arrive, give them a pencil and a "Resume" handout. Have them fill out a "resume." Have kids introduce themselves by explaining what they wrote.

2. Want ads—Hand out newspaper classified ads. Have kids look at the jobs advertised. Give each person paper and a pencil, and have them each write a personal "want ad" for their life. For example:

Wanted

funny, outgoing teenager wants peace, fulfillment and purpose in life. Hard worker. Will travel.

Have kids read and explain their want ads.

Tell kids the meeting's theme is working part time. Ask how many work part time. Form small groups of kids with jobs and kids who don't have jobs.

3. Punching a time clock—Tell kids to imagine their schedule as a time clock. Give each person a "Time Clock" handout and a pencil. Have kids follow the instructions on the handout.

After everyone has finished, have kids discuss any discrepancies in

Materials:
☐ spatulas
☐ small bean bags

For each person:
☐ pencil
☐ copy of "Resume" handout; "Time Clock" handout; and "What to Look for in a Job" handout
☐ newspaper classified ads
☐ paper
☐ Bible

their handout answers. Have kids talk about their job experiences, and how jobs conflict with commitments such as school, homework, family, friends, hobbies, youth group, church and extracurricular activities.

4. A Word on work—Form small groups and give each person a Bible. Assign each group one of these passages:

- Proverbs 16:3
- Matthew 20:1-16
- John 6:27-29
- Matthew 5:13-16
- Matthew 21:28-31a
- Ephesians 2:8-10

Have groups each read aloud their passage and discuss:

● **What, if anything, does this say about how you spend your time—on or off the job?**

● **What truths do these scriptures tell students who are juggling tons of commitments?**

After the discussion, ask each group to sing what it learned to the tune of "I've Been Workin' on the Railroad." Applaud jobs well-done! Then pray that God guides them in their decision whether to work part time.

5. Working advice—Have kids read "What to Look for in a Job." Have each person tell what he or she would add to the list of what to look for. If possible, invite an employer to come and tell teenagers what they should know about the working world—good and bad.

6. The fast-food phase—Order out for pizza. While you're waiting for it to arrive, play zany games as takeoffs on jobs kids have. For example, have a burger-flip contest with spatulas and bean bags to see how many flips a person can make in 30 seconds. Name the winner your "Burger King"!

Bonus Ideas!

● Visit an employment agency and hear about out-of-the-ordinary job options.

● Invite special speakers who hold unusual jobs to your group.

● Visit kids in their work places (without disrupting). Find out what they deal with at work.

● Order the article "What to Do With Kids Who Work" in the September 1984 issue of GROUP Magazine from Group Publishing, Box 481, Loveland, CO 80539.

Resume

Full Name: _____   Date of Birth: _____

Address: _____   Phone: _____

_____   S.S.#: _____

_____

Education: _____

_____

Extracurricular activities and awards: _____

_____

_____

Previous work experience (include name of business, address and length of employment):

_____

_____

_____

_____

_____

_____

_____

_____

Permission to photocopy this handout granted for local church use. Copyright © 1990 by Thom Schultz Publications, Inc., Box 481, Loveland, CO 80539.

Time Clock

Instructions: List on the handout all the commitments you have, how much time you spend for each and how much you'd like to spend for each.

Commitments	Time I spend	Time I'd like to spend

Permission to photocopy this handout granted for local church use. Copyright © 1990 by Thom Schultz Publications, Inc., Box 481, Loveland, CO 80539.

What to Look for in a Job

What advice would you give friends who're looking for jobs? Here's how some other teenagers responded to that question:

"Find something you think you'd enjoy. Then find out what kind of schedule you could get that would fit in with your schedule."
Melissa Hogston, 17, Boiling Springs, North Carolina

"Make sure you still have time for yourself and your friends. And don't let anyone take advantage of you just because you're a teenager."
Marisa Anderson, 17, Sonoma, California

"In some jobs you've got to be faster, and in some jobs you've got to be more polite. So find a place to work that fits your skills and personality."
Terry Wheeler, 17, Waco, Texas

"Don't work in a fast-food place. And don't work more than 15 hours a week. With five classes, it's hard to work more than that."
Laura Hamrick, 17, Boiling Springs, North Carolina

"Ask people where they work. If you're going to put in an application someplace, ask someone who works there about the job before you take it."
Brian Hof, 16, Grandview, Missouri

Permission to photocopy this handout granted for local church use. Copyright © 1990 by Thom Schultz Publications, Inc., Box 481, Loveland, CO 80539.

14. Overcoming the Fear of Failure

Purpose:
To help group members understand that it's better to take a risk and fail than never try at all.

Session outline:

1. Blowing it—Hand out balloons. Tell kids you'll give a prize to the person who blows up the biggest balloon without popping it. Let them try. Award bubble gum for the prize. Then ask:

● **How did you feel about this contest?**

● **Did some of you not even try? Why?**

● **How did you feel if your balloon popped in your face?**

Compare the feelings of kids who didn't try with kids who tried and failed.

2. I don't want to blow it—Have kids brainstorm things teenagers might be afraid to try because of the fear of failing; for example, trying out for a sports team, taking a public speaking class or taking the driving exam to get a license. List kids' responses on newsprint taped to a wall. Then give each person paper and a pencil, and have kids each rank the items according to what scares them most. Form groups of four and have kids tell why they rated the items the way they did.

3. One step at a time—With kids still in their groups, have them each choose something they're afraid to try and write it on a 3×5 card. For example, someone might be afraid to try out for a school

Materials:
☐ bubble gum
☐ tape
☐ newsprint
☐ marker
☐ Bible
☐ David Meece's album, *Chronology* (Word)

For each person:
☐ balloon
☐ paper
☐ pencil
☐ 3×5 card

play, write an article for the school newspaper or run for class president. On the back of each 3×5 card, have groups write a recipe to help group members each do whatever they're afraid to try. For example, a recipe to try out for the school play might read:

1—Pray for courage!

2—Get a copy of the play and practice it at home.

3—Get advice from friends who've been to auditions.

4—Get a friend to go with you to sign up for auditions.

5—Do it!

4. Peter's steps—Have someone read aloud Matthew 14:25-30. Ask:

● **What risk did Peter take?**

● **How did he succeed? How did he fail?**

● **Do you think Peter is more of a success or failure in this passage? Why?**

Compare Peter to the other disciples who sat in the boat and didn't take a risk.

5. Supporting each other—Play the song "Falling Down" from David Meece's album, *Chronology* (or something similar). Find a volunteer who's willing to take a risk. Ask that person to stand and have the other kids sit in a circle around that person with their stocking feet touching his or her ankles and holding their arms straight out in front of them. If you have fewer than six kids, stand in a tight circle facing the one in the middle. Tell the volunteer to become a "mummy" by hugging himself or herself and fall into group members' arms. The kids surrounding the volunteer will support and roll him or her around the circle. Let different volunteers be in the center. Then ask:

● **What's good about risking?**

● **What's the worst thing that can happen when you take a risk?**

● **Which is better—to risk and fail, or to never risk at all? Why?**

Tell a story from your own life when you failed before your efforts led to success.

6. Help—Have someone read aloud Hebrews 12:1. Challenge kids to support each other in risk-taking and not giving up. Form pairs and have kids share what they wrote on their 3×5 cards in activity #3. Ask kids to pray that God will give their partners the courage and faith to risk.

Bonus Ideas!

● **Counselor**—Invite a counselor who works with people who feel like failures. Have kids interview the counselor and discuss how people handle failure. Ask how people can be negatively and positively motivated by failure.

● **Risks**—Take the group on "risky" outings. For instance, go white-water rafting, rappelling or water skiing. Talk about why risks are both exciting and scary. Relate your activity to taking risks in school.

SECTION THREE:

Faith Issues

15. What's Up, God?

Purpose:

To help kids examine the importance of listening to God and how he speaks to us.

Session outline:

1. Before the meeting—Gather radios or two or three tape players and tapes. As kids arrive, play the radios or tape players loud enough so everyone has to shout over them to be heard clearly.

2. Casual conversations—Form small groups. With the radios or tape players still blaring, have someone from each group read "What's Up, God?" to his or her group. Afterward, turn off the noise and gather as a large group.

Ask:

● **What did your group reader say?**

● **What was it like to try to hear above all the noise?**

● **Did you understand most of the words? Why or why not?**

● **What did you do to try to hear better?**

3. Once again, but quietly—Reread "What's Up, God?" to the group. Ask:

● **How is listening to God like listening to your group reader through all the noise?**

● **How is listening to God like listening to me read when everything was quiet?**

● **Which experience was most like your communication with God?**

Materials:
☐ radios or two or three tapes and tape players
☐ markers
☐ newsprint
☐ masking tape
☐ cupcake
☐ birthday candle
☐ matches

For each small group:
☐ copy of "What's Up, God?" handout

For each person:
☐ paper
☐ pencil
☐ Bible

Read aloud 1 Kings 19:11-12. Have kids brainstorm other distractions that keep people from hearing God. List these on a large sheet of newsprint and tape it to the wall.

4. God speaks through the Bible—Form the same small groups. Give paper, a pencil and a Bible to each person and assign one of the following scripture passages to each group:

- Exodus 3:1-12
- Matthew 4:1-11
- Mark 4:35-41
- Luke 10:25-37
- John 2:13-17
- John 13:1-20

Have the members of each group read their scripture passage and then "place themselves in the Bible." Have them list what they feel, hear, taste, smell and see as if they were the Bible character.

Have each group describe its Bible passage from the first-person perspective for the rest of the groups. (For example: I was chasing one of my sheep back to the flock one day when suddenly a lone bush began to burn. Out of curiosity I decided to check it out . . .) Give groups the option of performing a role play while describing the scene and feelings. Ask:

- **Is it easy to place yourself in the Bible "with your feelings"? Why or why not?**
- **How does reading the Bible this way help you hear God?**

5. Overcoming distractions—Hand out sheets of newsprint and masking tape. Then have groups go around the room and cover distracting items (such as radios, posters and doorways) with paper and tape. Then distribute markers and ask group members to walk around the room and list—on the newsprint that covers the distractions—ways God speaks to them; for example, through prayer, scripture, other people.

6. Time out to listen—Say: **God's voice can get crowded out by all the stuff that fills our lives. That's why it's important to take some time out.**

You can take time out for God by:

- **praying;**
- **stopping and listening after you pray to hear if God has anything to say; or**
- **taking a long walk and imagining that Christ walks with you. For example, imagine what Jesus is saying to you. Or imagine he's simply walking with you in loving silence.**

Learning to listen to your heart as well as your head is the first step to hearing God's voice in your life.

Place a cupcake with a birthday candle in it on the floor. Gather kids in a circle around it. Turn out the lights and light the candle. Have kids take time to pray and then listen for God's answers while the candle burns. When the candle burns down to the cupcake, close with prayer asking God to help us take time to listen to him through prayer, the Bible and our hearts.

Bonus Ideas!

● **Time for listening**—Arrange to have each meeting open with a brief time of silent praying and listening to God.

● **Walk with God**—Take your group on a hike in the mountains, at the beach or in the woods. Ask kids to spend the time in silent communion with the Lord instead of talking with one another. Have kids bring a lunch or snack. At a halfway point, stop for food and discuss the wonder of God. Read aloud Psalm 24:1-2 and ask kids what it's like to simply be quiet in the midst of God's creation. Finish the hike with a silent and prayerful return to the starting place.

What's Up, God?

In the Bible, God talks to people all the time. It seems you can't read more than a page or two without God having a personal conversation with somebody. God makes a personal appearance in Isaiah 6 to talk with Isaiah about his career as a prophet. God discusses with Abraham about whether or not to nuke Sodom in Genesis 18. And God gets a point across to Saul on the road to Damascus in Acts 9.

Even when God isn't talking directly to somebody in the Bible, you can find the apostles experiencing the Holy Spirit in Acts 2. Or you can read about somebody sharing a vision of God in great detail in the books of Revelation and Daniel.

But what about today? How does God talk to you?

Hearing God's voice is as simple as tuning a radio to your favorite channel. Once you've learned to tune in to God, you can receive God's message in the Bible, in music, in the voices of friends, in a sunset, in church, while riding in a car or while standing on your head.

How do you tune in to God? Start by clearing away some of the clutter in your life. Learn how to feel. All the biggies in the Bible, from Adam to John, heard God's voice by opening their heart and soul to God.

Permission to photocopy this handout granted for local church use. Copyright © 1990 by Thom Schultz Publications, Inc., Box 481, Loveland, CO 80539.

16. How Can I Know if God Loves Me?

Purpose:
To help kids understand that God loves them, and know how easy it is to accept that love.

Session outline:

1. What is love?—Brainstorm a definition of love with your group. Use 1 Corinthians 13 as a guide. Write the definition on a large paper heart and tape it to the wall. Then ask:

- **When you love someone, what do you do for them?**
- **Which word best describes love—"giving" or "receiving"? Explain.**

2. Looking for love—Before the meeting, place two small objects (such as buttons or thimbles) in plain sight in another room. Form two teams. Blindfold a volunteer from each team and take the volunteers and their teammates to the other room. Tell the blindfolded people they are each to find an object. Teammates may help direct their volunteer by using only a humming noise to indicate whether the person is hot or cold. (The louder the humming, the closer the person is to the object.) No one may talk. The first team to successfully direct its blindfolded teammate to pick up the object wins.

3. What does it mean?—Form a circle after the game. Ask the kids who were blindfolded:

- **How did it feel not to know where you were going?**

Materials:
- ☐ large paper heart
- ☐ marker
- ☐ two button or thimbles
- ☐ two blindfolds

For each person:
- ☐ Bible
- ☐ scissors
- ☐ marker
- ☐ piece of masking tape

● **Was it difficult to find the object? Why or why not?**

● **Could you have found the object without the help of the humming? Why or why not?**

Ask the other team members:

● **How did it feel to know where the object was and yet not be able to tell your teammate?**

● **How did the blindfold affect the person's ability to find the object?**

4. The object of God's love—Form small groups. Tell them to imagine that the object in the game represented God's love. Then ask:

● **Was there any proof to the blindfolded person that the object would be where it was found? Why or why not?**

● **Why did the blindfolded person keep searching for the item?**

5. The humming is really a shout—Give each person a Bible. Have groups look up the following verses: Isaiah 54:10; John 3:16; Romans 8:31-39; and Ephesians 2:3-6. Ask:

● **According to these scriptures, does God love you? Why?**

● **Is it really that simple? Why or why not?**

● **How is the written Word of God like the humming that helped the teenager find the object?**

● **How is the Bible a guide to help us find God's love?**

6. Heart to heart—Have each group member tear off a piece of the heart that has the definition of love on it. Distribute scissors and have each person cut that piece to form a smaller heart. Give teenagers each a marker and a piece of tape. Have them each write "God loves me" on the heart and tape the heart to another person while saying, "God loves you."

Bonus Ideas!

● **How big is God's love?**—Have kids write poems, stories, songs or skits that demonstrate how much God really loves us. Then ask for a set time during each regular worship service to have one of these descriptions of God's love read or performed for the whole congregation. Or have a special program devoted to the "bigness" of God's love.

● **"Wear it"**—Have the artistic ones in your group design T-shirts with words such as "I know God loves me" written on them. Sell them as a fund-raiser or give them away as prizes for regular group meeting contests.

17. Does God Really Answer My Prayers?

Purpose:
To discuss the importance of prayer.

Session outline:

1. Is anybody listening?—Ask group members to think about a personal prayer request they prayed about this past week. After giving kids a minute to think, say: **On "go," everyone say aloud your request.**

Say "go." After kids all talk at once, ask several kids to repeat what someone said from across the room. Then ask:

- **How is this like the way God hears our prayers? How is it different?**
- **Does God always answer prayer? Explain.**
- **How does he answer prayer?**

Have kids each say their prayer request again—one at a time. Explain that God hears us when we pray just as if we were the only person talking to him.

2. Prayer quiz—Have everyone do the "Who Prayed for What?" quiz. When everyone has finished, go over the answers by reading the scriptures listed on the handout.

Materials:

- [ ] paper
- [ ] marker
- [ ] masking tape
- [ ] soft instrumental music (optional)
- [ ] stereo (optional)

For each person:
- [ ] copy of "Who Prayed for What?" quiz; "Prayer Pointers" handout; "Prayer Request" handout; and "Prayer Jewels" handout
- [ ] pencil
- [ ] Bible

3. What is prayer?—Form pairs. Ask group members to think about their concerns and joys. Then give partners each two minutes to describe their concerns and joys. Encourage them to be as honest and natural as they would be in normal conversation with a friend.

Explain that prayer is like that kind of communication—talking with a friend. Read aloud "Pray to Abba" in the "Prayer Pointers" handout. Ask:

● **How would you tell a loving, accepting dad about your concerns, hopes and joys?**

4. An offer God can't refuse—Have kids read aloud the rest of the "Prayer Pointers" handout. Have group members come up with their own examples of prayers God can't resist.

Ask:

● **Why are these prayers important?**

5. Make a wish—Give each person a "Prayer Request" handout and have kids each complete it. Explain that one other person will be reading their requests later in the meeting. As kids finish, collect the sheets to use during the closing activity.

6. Silent, public prayers—In separate areas of the room, display a piece of paper with one of the following words: "Self," "School," "Family," "Others," "World Concerns." Then have a time of silent prayer. Ask group members to stand next to the appropriate sign as they talk silently with God about self, school, family, others or world concerns. If possible, play soft instrumental music during the silent-prayer time.

7. Biblical thoughts—Have group members sit in a circle and read aloud the "Prayer Jewels" handout and the following scripture passages: Psalm 145:18; Matthew 6:5-13; and James 5:13-18. Ask:

● **What do these scriptures tell us about God and how we should approach him in prayer?**

● **Are some prayers best kept "just between you and God"? Why or why not?**

● **What advantages do community (publicly spoken) prayers have?**

● **Is it helpful to have a prayer partner? Why or why not?**

8. Closing prayer—Distribute the "Prayer Request" handouts kids filled out earlier and allow group members to read them. Then close with a prayer asking God to help everyone know how to pray. Encourage teenagers each to take home their list and pray for that person each night this week.

Bonus Ideas!

● **Prayer night**—Sponsor an all-night prayer vigil for your church. Have congregation members and group members sign up for half-hour blocks of time throughout the night to come and pray. At the vigil, have lists of prayer requests available.

● **Read**—Get a copy of *Questions? Answers* by Verne Becker, Tim Stafford and Philip Yancey, (Tyndale House Publishers) and *Disappointment With God* by Philip Yancey (Zondervan Publishing House).

Who Prayed for What?

Instructions: Read the requests below and figure out who in the Bible prayed each one. Draw a line to match the request with the person. Who prayed:

● for his friends?

● that the thorn in his flesh be removed?

● for strength?

● "may this cup be taken from me"?

● in anger for the Lord to take his life away?

● about himself?

● Jonah (Jonah 4:1-4)

● The Pharisee (Luke 18:11)

● Job (Job 42:10)

● Paul (2 Corinthians 12:7-9)

● Samson (Judges 16:28)

● Jesus (Matthew 26:39, 42, 44)

Permission to photocopy this handout granted for local church use. Copyright © 1990 by Thom Schultz Publications, Inc., Box 481, Loveland, CO 80539.

Prayer Request

Instructions: In the space below, write your three most important prayer requests. Sign your name in the space provided.

Name: _____

My three most important prayer requests are:

1.

2.

3.

Permission to photocopy this handout granted for local church use. Copyright © 1990 by Thom Schultz Publications, Inc., Box 481, Loveland, CO 80539.

Prayer Pointers

So how should we pray? And what should we expect? Try these ideas:

● **Pray to Abba.** In the New Testament, this Aramaic word always gets translated "Father." But that's not an accurate translation. In the English language, we have many words for our male parent—Father, Dad, Daddy. The same is true in Aramaic.

So translate Abba as Daddy, or even Da Da. Jesus himself prayed to Abba. It's the most childlike and intimate of all prayer forms. And it best expresses how we should approach God.

● **Pray prayers you know God can't resist answering.** Then picture God hearing and responding.

Pray: "Lord, I want to learn your will. Could you help me?" or "I want to know how to be your child. Please help me."

When you're frustrated and don't know where to go for help, your only prayer may be, "God, love me." How could an Abba resist such a prayer?

● **Ask the Holy Spirit to pray for you.** Often we don't know what to ask or even hope for. When that happens to you, try sitting in silence, opening your hands before God and asking the Holy Spirit to lift up your life.

The most beautiful process of prayer—and of life—isn't getting what you ask for, but the process of day-by-day surrendering yourself to God's care, whether you understand it or not. Through this process, the realization grows. God always answers prayer—maybe not in the way you'd always like him to. But he *always* answers prayer.

Permission to photocopy this handout granted for local church use. Copyright © 1990 by Thom Schultz Publications, Inc., Box 481, Loveland, CO 80539.

Prayer Jewels

"In the same way, the Spirit helps us, in our weakness. We do not know what we ought to pray for, but the Spirit himself intercedes for us with groans that words cannot express" (Romans 8:26).

"But I tell you: Love your enemies and pray for those who persecute you" (Matthew 5:44).

"I pray to you, O Lord, in the time of your favor; in your great love, O God, answer me with your sure salvation" (Psalm 69:13).

"He said to them, 'When you pray, say: "Father, hallowed be your name, your kingdom come. Give us each day our daily bread. Forgive us our sins, for we also forgive everyone who sins against us. And lead us not into temptation' " (Luke 11:2-4).

"Is any one of you in trouble? He should pray. Is anyone happy? Let him sing songs of praise" (James 5:13).

"Pray continually" (1 Thessalonians 5:17).

Permission to photocopy this handout granted for local church use. Copyright © 1990 by Thom Schultz Publications, Inc., Box 481, Loveland, CO 80539.

18. Is the "Good Book" Any Good?

Purpose:
To explore the Bible's relevance for today.

Session outline:

1. Good-Booking it—Do this relay in which kids really have to "book." Use a large room or hallway. Form two teams. Have them line up side by side. Team members must, one at a time, "book" to the other end of the room and unstack and stack, one by one, a pile of assorted books. Include poetry, fiction, history and schoolbooks of various sizes. Have the same number of books in each team's pile. If you like, award the winning team members gift certificates to a Christian bookstore.

Have everyone sit in a circle around the books. Ask which are "good books." Let kids tell why they like certain types of books.

2. Getting into it—Invite kids to tell ways they hear people "use" the Bible. For example, opening it and expecting a random verse to give direction. Discuss comments.

Ask:

● **What if a suicidal person randomly opened the Bible to**

Materials:
- ☐ two stacks of assorted books
- ☐ bookstore gift certificate (optional)
- ☐ paper
- ☐ marker
- ☐ newsprint
- ☐ tape
- ☐ copy of "A Guidebook" handout

For each person:
- ☐ blank paper bookmark
- ☐ marker
- ☐ Bible

Matthew 27:5 ("Then he went away and hanged himself")?

3. Translation of truths—Form four groups. Give each group a piece of paper with the following verses listed on it:

- Matthew 5:13-16
- Matthew 13:45-46
- Luke 14:1-6
- Matthew 13:31-32
- Luke 12:35-40

Have groups use the following four-step process to identify and understand these scriptures' timeless meanings. Write the process on newsprint and tape it to a wall:

1) Read the passage.

2) Identify the elements of the passage that relate specifically to the culture of the time. (Have Bible commentaries available as resources.)

3) Determine the key principle the passage is trying to get across.

4) Reword the passage using cultural elements from today's society. For example, "I am the vine, you are the branches" might become "I am the main computer and you are the terminals."

4. A mark to remember—Have groups report two or three of their reworded passages. Hand out blank paper bookmarks and markers. Have kids each pick their favorite reworded passage (with the scripture reference) and write it on the bookmark. Suggest they use these bookmarks in their own Bibles.

5. Using the guidebook—Stay in the same four groups. Assign each a part of the "A Guidebook" handout. Have groups each read the Bible passage in their section and discuss the Bible's guidance on their topic. Then have them explain the Bible's message, in their own words, to the whole group.

6. The next step—Give kids a moment to think about how they might make the Bible more meaningful to them. Have them write a one-line prayer on the back of their bookmarks that asks God to help them see the relevance of the Bible for their lives.

7. Closing—Have kids each hold a Bible in their hands during the prayer. Ask God to make the Bible come alive to the group and to help everyone look more closely at what the Bible has to say.

KEEP GOING!

Bonus Ideas!

● **Newsworthy Bibles**—Design a meeting around the daily newspaper. Supply newspapers for the group. Divide the pages among group members. Have them use concordances to find scripture passages that apply to each story or ad—from front-page disasters to entertainment. Discuss discoveries made through the experience.

● **The "Word"-shop**—Hold a day-long workshop on how to study the Bible. Include different study methods and sample studies that your workshop team does together.

● **Faith record**—The Bible records the Israelites' faith walk with God. Why not record your group's faith walk? Let group members organize and create a journal of personal and group faith-experiences. For example, write stories, poems, songs, allegories. Periodically examine the journal together to focus on faith discoveries.

● **Other issues and topics**—Have kids list other topics they'd like guidance on but haven't found in the Bible; for example, drugs. Tell kids you'll take the list and note Bible references that relate to those topics and give references to them a week or so later. Meet with the pastor and others if necessary to find passages with principles that apply. Then tell group members how you found the passages so they can learn to do the same thing.

● **Good books about the Good Book**—Look into *Dennis Benson's Creative Bible Studies: Matthew—Acts* and *Dennis Benson's Creative Bible Studies: Romans—Revelation*, by Dennis Benson (Group Books). Also check out *Fun Old Testament Bible Studies* by Mike Gillespie (also by Group Books). The book contains 32 involving studies on Old Testament personalities and stories.

A Guidebook

Instructions: Photocopy this handout and cut apart the sections. Give each section to a different group and have group members discuss it.

✂ -

- **On getting caught**—You can't get more ancient than Adam and Eve. In *Genesis 3*, they chose to disobey God, and they immediately felt embarrassed and guilty. When they heard their Creator walking around in the garden, they hid themselves. When God found them, God asked Adam why they were hiding. Adam said he felt afraid because he was naked. Have you ever felt embarrassed and afraid when you were caught doing something you knew was wrong?

- -

- **On peer pressure**—You're at a party and the beer is flowing like Niagara Falls. A friend offers you a drink. Enter: peer pressure!
  What does the Bible say about peer pressure? More than you think. Look at Aaron in *Exodus 32*, for example. He got stuck with a lot of restless people while his brother Moses had been gone a long time. The people wanted some religious action. Aaron, who was left in charge, knew that things were getting out of hand. The people asked Aaron to make an idol for them to worship instead of worshiping God. Enter: peer pressure!

- -

- **On AIDS**—Jesus encountered a group of people considered unclean and untouchable in *Luke 17:11-19*. They had a highly contagious disease called leprosy, which many people believed was caused by sin. Jesus treated these people with compassion, and on several occasions physically touched them.
  In some ways, AIDS victims are today's lepers. Yes, many who have the disease contracted it because they chose a high-risk lifestyle. But others who suffer from this disease contracted it innocently. The Bible encourages us to be like Jesus, who touched the untouchable and loved the unlovable.

- -

- **On rock music**—There was a problem in Corinth. In *1 Corinthians 8*, we read about some church people buying and eating meat that had been offered to idols. Other people thought that was bad news. They said people buying and eating that meat approved of idol worship.
  Today some Christians think listening to contemporary Christian artists such as Stryper, Petra, and DeGarmo & Key is like worshiping idols. They're convinced that rock music—Christian or otherwise—is evil. But other Christians disagree. They feel Christian musicians sing worthwhile songs.
  Read *1 Corinthians 8* to get Paul's solution to the problem.

Permission to photocopy this handout granted for local church use. Copyright © 1990 by Thom Schultz Publications, Inc., Box 481, Loveland, CO 80539.

19. Tackling Spirituality

Purpose:
To explore spiritual growth using a football-season theme.

Session outline:

1. Football follies—Have marching-band music playing as kids arrive. Create a relay with two sets of football paraphernalia such as helmets, shoulder pads, a uniform, a football. Form two teams and designate two ends of the room as goal lines. Then divide each team in half with one half at each goal. Have one person from each team don the football gear and carry a football to the other half of the team. At that time the person takes off the gear and has another teammate put it on and carry the ball back to the other half of the team. Do this until each person has put on the gear. Tell teams to cheer each other with football cheers. Award all the players with popcorn and soft drinks.

Materials:
- ☐ marching-band music
- ☐ stereo
- ☐ two football uniforms
- ☐ two footballs
- ☐ popcorn
- ☐ soft drinks
- ☐ copy of "Tackling Tough Times" handout; "Huddling Together" handout; "Supporting the Team" handout; and "Playing Your Position" handout

For each small group:
- ☐ Bibles
- ☐ pencils

2. Forming a spiritual team—Form four teams. Explain how growing spiritually can be compared to football practice. Ask football enthusiasts to give examples.

Choose a "football captain" to lead each team. If possible, have an adult be on each team too. Give each team Bibles, pencils and one of the following handouts:
- "Tackling Tough Times"

- "Huddling Together"
- "Supporting the Team"
- "Playing Your Position"

Have teams each complete their handout.

3. Celebrate a victory—Gather the teams together and discuss what they learned. As a sign of affirmation for each team player, have kids one by one be lifted above everybody's shoulders as the group cheers that person's name.

Bonus Ideas!

● **"One another" scripture search**—Give each person paper, a Bible and a pencil. Give kids 10 minutes to find as many verses that refer to "one another" or "each other" as they can. Here are some examples: Romans 12:10; Ephesians 4:2, 32; 5:21; Colossians 3:16; 1 Thessalonians 4:18; James 5:16; and 1 John 1:7.

Ask:

● **What patterns do you see among these verses?**
● **Which verses mean the most to you? Why?**

● **Spiritual teammates**—Have kids form pairs to pray for each other every day for a week. Every day each partner should find a scripture verse that's extra special to him or her and "hand off" that verse to his or her partner. The next week form new partnerships. Watch your group members grow by praying for one another.

● **Video bonanza**—Get the *Champions* video curriculum resource (Word). Arrange a two-part series as a time to strengthen your spiritual youth group team by learning from Christian athletes.

● **Spiritual growth resources**—Stock your library shelves with these books: *Adolescent Spirituality* by Charles Shelton (Loyola University Press); *Faith Shaping* by Stephen Jones (Judson Press); and *The Power of Encouragement* by Jeanne Doering (Moody Press).

Tackling Tough Times

John dreamed of becoming a football player, but he didn't want to practice. After a month, he became discouraged. John started to bobble passes. He fumbled the ball. He botched easy plays. And at times he wanted to quit.

Many of us want to become strong Christians, but we don't want to practice. Yet it's a lifelong process to become a strong Christian. We need to go to church, read our Bibles, pray and get together with other Christians. This is "practice." Practice makes Christians strong.

"Let us throw off everything that hinders . . . and let us run with perseverance the race marked out for us" (Hebrews 12:1b).

Think of a specific goal that will help you become a strong Christian. For example, "To take part in a Bible study with other Christians that begins next Wednesday and continues for eight weeks." Write it below, and share it with your teammates. Choose someone on your team to help hold you accountable to strive for your goal.

Your goal: _____

_____

_____

_____

_____

Start-up date: _____

How often you'll do this: _____

Who'll hold you accountable: _____

Permission to photocopy this handout granted for local church use. Copyright © 1990 by Thom Schultz Publications, Inc., Box 481, Loveland, CO 80539.

Huddling Together

For a football team to carry out a play effectively, it has to huddle together. Each team player needs to know what each other player is doing, so he can work with the rest of the team to gain yards—and eventually win the game.

Christians need each other. So huddle with your teammates to read a few verses of the Bible daily. Hold each other accountable. Encourage each other to keep reading the Bible. Discuss each day's reading.

"But encourage one another daily, as long as it is called Today" (Hebrews 3:13a).

Your Pact

Decide how many verses each person on your team will read each day. Then hold each other accountable. Encourage each other by calling during the week or meeting together to discuss what you've read.

Person who'll hold you accountable: _____

Number of verses you'll read daily: _____

Permission to photocopy this handout granted for local church use. Copyright © 1990 by Thom Schultz Publications, Inc., Box 481, Loveland, CO 80539.

Supporting the Team

What makes a team come back after a bad season? Answer: A good coach.

When your friends have a "bad season," encourage them. Don't judge them. Pat them on the back. Help them get back on their feet. Encourage them to do good, love others and love God.

"And let us consider how we may spur one another on toward love and good deeds" (Hebrews 10:24).

It's tough when you and your friends get discouraged. But don't give up. Try these lifter-uppers to keep going. Checkmark each one that your team will do for someone this week.

☐ Make a batch of brownies.

☐ Kidnap a friend and have a picnic on the high school parking lot.

☐ Get travel posters from a local travel agency of your friend's favorite vacation spots. Hang them on your friend's bedroom walls or locker.

☐ Wake your friend early to watch a sunrise with you.

☐ Serenade your friend outside his or her bedroom window.

☐ Other _____

Permission to photocopy this handout granted for local church use. Copyright © 1990 by Thom Schultz Publications, Inc., Box 481, Loveland, CO 80539.

Playing Your Position

A football team has many players: quarterbacks, fullbacks, defensive backs, linemen and receivers. Every player masters a different position, and a team needs every player. To score a touchdown, players need to work together as a team.

Your youth group is like a football team. Each member has different spiritual gifts, and your youth group needs each member. To become a strong Christian, work with other Christians as a team. Encourage and coach each other.

"The body is a unit, though it is made up of many parts . . . Now you are the body of Christ, and each one of you is a part of it" (1 Corinthians 12:12, 27).

In the roster below, list the names of your youth group team members. Then write what position each person plays. Pray for your teammates and thank God for each individual's gift.

Name	Position
Example: Candice	Receiver: She always welcomes me.

Permission to photocopy this handout granted for local church use. Copyright © 1990 by Thom Schultz Publications, Inc., Box 481, Loveland, CO 80539.

20. "Do I Have to Go to Church?"

Purpose:

To help group members change their thinking from "What do I get from church?" to "What can I give to church?"

Session outline:

1. Excuse-a-thon—Form teams. Challenge teams to list on paper as many excuses as possible for not going to church. Have teams act out the excuses for the others to guess. Have kids vote for the wildest excuse, the most unbelievable excuse, and the most believable excuse.

2. Bible thoughts—Have someone read aloud Luke 14:15-24. Ask:

● **What are the three excuses in the parable?**

● **What did the three people miss out on because they didn't go to the banquet?**

● **What didn't they get to give by not going to the banquet?**

Have someone read aloud Exodus 20:8-11 and Hebrews 10:25. Ask:

● **What do these verses say about why we should go to church?**

Materials:

☐ newsprint
☐ marker
☐ cookies
☐ decorating gel

For each small group:
☐ large box
☐ construction paper
☐ scissors
☐ tape
☐ markers
☐ paper

For each person:
☐ pencil
☐ 3×5 card
☐ copy of "Your Church's Job Description" handout
☐ Bible

- **Why is the Sabbath so important?**
- **Why is worshiping with other Christians so important?**
- **What's worship? Explain.**

3. The ideal church—Form small groups. Give each group a large box, construction paper, scissors, tape, markers, paper and pencils. Tell groups each to design the ideal church—based on the excuses they heard for people to not attend church. Say each small group should create:

(1) the church building; and

(2) an "ideal" worship service.

They may include serious and zany elements. Each group might make some element of its building or worship service solve the problem that "church is boring." For example, a church sanctuary may have 20 TV screens and large speakers for contemporary Christian music videos. Have groups explain their ideal churches and worship services to the whole group.

4. Job description—Have kids each complete the first half of the "Your Church's Job Description" handout.

5. Our church—Have group members look at what they wrote and brainstorm real suggestions for how they'd like to see their church change. List them on newsprint. Add ideas for how kids can help the changes happen. Plan to give the list to your pastor or appropriate church board.

6. Commitment to give—Choose the church building created in activity #3 that most closely resembles your church. Have kids do the second half of "Your Church's Job Description" and each write on a 3×5 card one talent or skill they'll use to improve church. Have kids put the cards inside the small church building.

7. Closing—Close with a prayer asking God to help people ask what they can give to their church rather than what they can get from it.

8. No-excuse cookies—Provide cookies and decorating gel for writing. Let kids write on the cookies excuses for not attending church. Then let them get rid of the excuses by eating them!

Bonus Ideas!

- **Ideas**—All group members can attend the appropriate church board meeting to present their serious ideas for changing the church.
- **Cookie-baking**—Bake the "no-excuse cookies" together during your meeting.

Your Church's Job Description

Instructions: In the space below, write a job description for your church. Rank its five major job responsibilities. Read these Bible passages to get you started:

- Psalm 95:6-7
- Psalm 133:1
- Proverbs 29:18
- John 5:39
- 1 Corinthians 13:3

- Psalm 118:24
- Proverbs 18:24
- Matthew 10:8, 34
- Romans 12:10
- 1 John 4:7

Your church's job responsibilities:

1.

2.

3.

4.

5.

Now imagine you're applying for a job at your church. Rank your five top talents or skills and write them below.

My five top talents or skills:

1.

2.

3.

4.

5.

Now match your skills with the five most important job responsibilities of the church. Do any match? If so, congratulations. You get the job!

What skills can you give to meet your church's job requirements? Volunteer your services and get busy. You and your church may need each other more than you think.

Permission to photocopy this handout granted for local church use. Copyright © 1990 by Thom Schultz Publications, Inc., Box 481, Loveland, CO 80539.